Festivals of the World

UKRAINE

Gareth Stevens Publishing
MILWAUKEE

Written by
VLADIMIR BASSIS

Edited by
NURUL AIN BTE ABD KARIM

Designed by
HASNAH MOHD ESA

Picture research by
SUSAN JANE MANUEL

First published in North America in 1998 by
Gareth Stevens Publishing
1555 North RiverCenter Drive, Suite 201
Milwaukee, Wisconsin 53212 USA

For a free color catalog describing Gareth
Stevens' list of high-quality books and multimedia
programs, call
1-800-542-2595 (USA)
or 1-800-461-9120 (Canada).
Gareth Stevens Publishing's Fax: (414) 225-0377.
See our catalog, too, on the World Wide Web:
http://gsinc.com

© TIMES EDITIONS PTE LTD 1998
Originated and designed by
Times Books International
an imprint of Times Editions Pte Ltd
Times Centre, 1 New Industrial Road
Singapore 536196
Printed in Singapore

Library of Congress Cataloging-in-Publication Data:
Bassis, Vladimir.
Ukraine / by Vladimir Bassis.
p. cm.—(Festivals of the world)
Includes bibliographical references and indexes.
Summary: Describes how the culture of Ukraine is
reflected in its many festivals, including Yumoryna,
Ivana Kupala, and Old New Year.
ISBN 0-8368-2010-X (lib. bdg.)
1. Festivals—Ukraine—Juvenile literature. 2.
Ukraine—Social life and customs—Juvenile
literature. [1. Festivals—Ukraine. 2. Holidays—
Ukraine. 3. Ukraine—Social life and customs.] I.
Title. II. Series.
GT4856.3.A2B37 1998
394.269477—dc21   97-38138

1 2 3 4 5 6 7 8 9 02 01 00 99 98

CONTENTS

It's Festival Time . . .

The Ukrainian word for festival is *sviato* [SVIA-toh]. For many years, Ukrainians were not allowed to celebrate their sviato. There were fears that many of their traditions would be lost. But today, Ukrainians are celebrating festivals the way they have been for generations. So, come along and jump over a bonfire, dress up as a ghost for Christmas, or decorate a New Year tree. It's festival time in Ukraine . . .

WHERE'S UKRAINE?

U kraine is one of the largest countries in Europe in terms of land and population. Ukraine's neighbors are Russia and Belarus to the east and north; Poland, Slovakia, and Hungary to the west; and Romania and Moldova to the south. The Black Sea borders half of southern Ukraine.

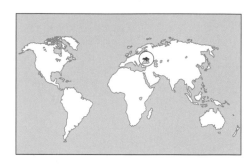

Ukraine is divided into 25 states, called *oblasts* [OB-lahsts]. The capital is Kiev.

Who are the Ukrainians?

The city of Kiev recently celebrated its 1,500th anniversary, but archaeological excavations show evidence of a civilization that dates as far back as 10,000 years ago. Russia, Belarus, and Ukraine used to make up one country called Kievan Rus. It was the cradle of civilization for all Eastern **Slavic** nations. Because of its rich farmlands, Ukraine was often invaded by outside forces. In 1991, Ukraine became independent. Ukrainians are proud of their independence.

Traditional Ukrainian dress
is bright and colorful.

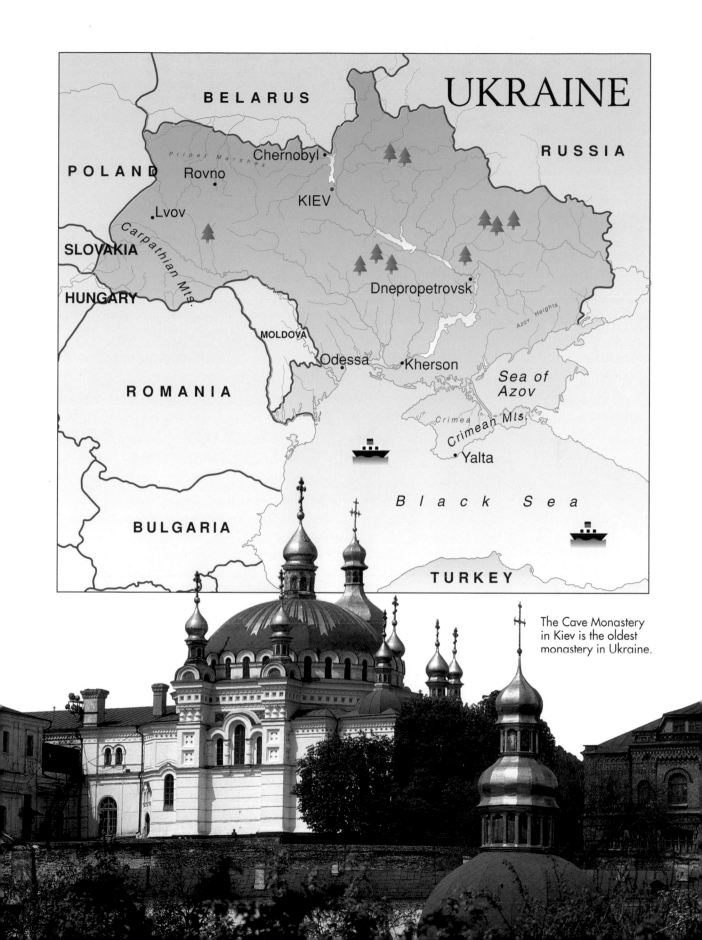

UKRAINE

BELARUS

POLAND

Pripet Marshes

Chernobyl

Rovno

RUSSIA

Lvov

KIEV

Carpathian Mts.

SLOVAKIA

HUNGARY

MOLDOVA

Dnepropetrovsk

Azov Heights

ROMANIA

Odessa

Kherson

Sea of Azov

Crimea *Crimean Mts.*

Yalta

Black Sea

BULGARIA

TURKEY

The Cave Monastery in Kiev is the oldest monastery in Ukraine.

WHEN'S THE SVIATO?

SPRING

- **INTERNATIONAL WOMEN'S DAY**—On March 8th, wives, mothers, and sisters are honored by husbands, fathers, and brothers with flowers and gifts.
- **EASTER**
- **YUMORYNA**—A festival of humor that takes place in Odessa each year on April 1st. Highlights include a carnival parade, concerts, plays, masquerades, humor contests, and an antique car parade.
- **MAY 1ST**—Traditionally, this holiday has been associated with spring, although it is also International Workers' Day. Today, people in Ukraine enjoy May 1st as a day for fun, relaxation, and picnics.

- **VICTORY DAY**—Victory Day is celebrated on May 9th. Every town has a memorial dedicated to the soldiers who died during World War II. People bring flowers to the memorials and honor war veterans.

SUMMER

- **IVANA KUPALA**
- **INDEPENDENCE DAY**—August 24th is Independence Day in Ukraine. The Ukrainian Parliament proclaimed independence from the Soviet Union on this day in 1991. People celebrate this official holiday with fireworks, parades, and festive food.

I make it look easy, but it's actually very difficult to play this instrument.

Sing along to the music! It's time to let your hair down and really party!

AUTUMN

✪ **THE DAY OF KNOWLEDGE**—The first day of the school year, September 1st, is called the Day of Knowledge in Ukraine. Students bring flowers to school and honor their teachers. This day is also often called Teachers' Day.

✪ **THE HARVEST FESTIVAL**

WINTER

✪ **NEW YEAR'S EVE**
✪ **CHRISTMAS**
✪ **OLD NEW YEAR**
✪ **WATER BLESSING CEREMONY**

WINTER FESTIVALS

Almost all the winter festivals in Ukraine take place within the month of January. January 1st is New Year's Day, January 7th is Christmas, January 14th commemorates Old New Year, and the Water Blessing Ceremony is held on January 18th. With all this fun going on, it is impossible to study! Ukrainian schoolchildren have their winter break for ten days beginning January 1st.

Adults dress up in funny costumes for Old New Year.

Riding a sled through the neighborhood on Old New Year's Eve.

All night long

The New Year celebration is probably the most popular holiday in Ukraine. It is the occasion for the longest party of the year—all night long! To prepare for the holiday, the house must be decorated. The main decoration is the New Year tree. It can be a pine or a fir tree. It is put up several days before New Year's Eve and decorated with colorful glass and plastic ornaments. Strings of lights are hung around the tree and throughout the house. Some people even hang candies and cookies on the tree, but no one is allowed to touch them before New Year comes! After the New Year tree is decorated, it's time for the party!

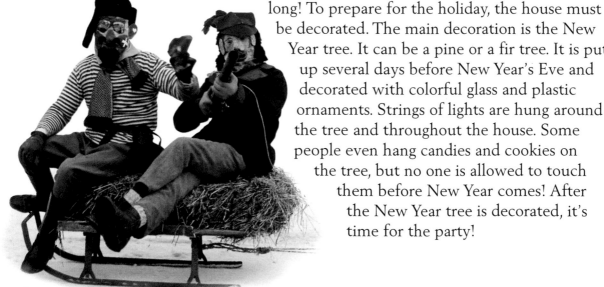

8

Children put on a
special play on
New Year's Day.

Party time!

People gather for a New Year's party as early as nine or ten o'clock
on New Year's Eve. Before the clock strikes midnight, all the guests
help prepare the festive table for the hungry crowds. At midnight,
everyone says goodbye to the old year and greets the new year. This
is when the party begins! Fireworks are set off outside in the yard,
while eating, drinking, and all kinds of fun and games take place
inside. The party can go on all night long and, as an exception to
the general rule, children are allowed to stay up for as long as they
can keep from falling asleep!

Left: Bringing the water home after it has been blessed.

Below: A Ukrainian **Orthodox** priest leans down to bless the water.

Old New Year

According to the old Ukrainian calendar, New Year comes on January 14th. Today, this day is called Old New Year. On Old New Year's Eve, children gather in groups and go from house to house wishing people prosperity in the coming year. They recite a special set of rhymes and sing songs just for the occasion. This is called *schedrivka* [sched-REEV-kah], which means "generosity," because in exchange for the wishes of wealth and health, the residents of each house must provide gifts, candies, and food.

The Water Blessing Ceremony

Ukrainians gather at the edge of a stream for the Water Blessing Ceremony.

On January 18th, Ukrainians from across the country gather at rivers, lakes, and churches for the annual Water Blessing Ceremony. Pots, pails, jars, and bowls are filled with water and brought to the ceremonial areas to be blessed by a priest. The priest dresses in special robes for this occasion. Once everyone has gathered, he recites scriptures over the water to make it holy. Afterward, the water is brought home and families enjoy a huge festive meal.

Think about this

The New Year celebration is one of the most important festivals of the year. People make resolutions and hope each year will be better than the last. Many Ukrainians believe that a wish made the moment the New Year arrives will come true during the coming year. Are there special beliefs connected with New Year where you live? What are they?

EASTER

J ust like many other holidays in Ukraine, the Easter celebrations combine Christian and pre-Christian traditions. In Ukraine, Easter is primarily dedicated to Christ's Resurrection, but it also embraces the joy associated with the arrival of spring and the revival of nature. Easter is

Carrying a lighted candle to celebrate Easter.

celebrated according to the old church calendar, but it is always in spring, when trees are turning green and the first flowers start to appear.

Forty days before Easter

The Easter season starts 40 days before Easter Sunday with the beginning of Lent. Traditionally, no meat or animal fats were allowed during Lent. During Holy Week, the week before Easter, milk, cheese, and oils weren't allowed either. People believed a strict fast was essential to cleanse themselves before the greatest event of the year—Easter.

Today, Ukrainians repair, whitewash, and clean their houses, and select their best clothes to wear on Easter Sunday.

Children look into the baskets of food blessed by the priest.

Easter traditions

Several special church services are conducted during the days of preparation before Easter. On Palm Sunday, people carry a single branch of pussy willow. On meeting, friends tap each other with the branch, saying: "It is not me who tapped you, but the willow."

Good Friday is called Passion Friday in Ukraine, and for two days, special church services are conducted. Huge amounts of festive food are prepared in every home. Among the more common are ham, sausages, cheese, and butter. The traditional Ukrainian Easter bread, **Paska**, is a rich, round loaf of bread decorated with elaborate dough ornaments that symbolize prosperity. Hard-boiled eggs painted in different colors are also a traditional part of the festive Easter table.

Orthodox priests conduct an Easter service. A huge loaf of Paska on a gold embroidered cloth will soon be blessed.

Ukrainian Easter eggs come in all patterns and colors. The traditional Ukrainian colors are red and black.

The art of pysanka

There are two kinds of Ukrainian Easter eggs. *Krashanka* [KRAH-shahn-kah], which means "painted," are colored hard-boiled eggs with a simple design. Traditional Ukrainian Easter eggs are called *pysanka* [PIH-sahn-kah], from the old Ukrainian word meaning "to decorate with painting." Unlike krashanka, pysanka are not eaten; they are exchanged as presents on Easter and sometimes kept for generations. According to Ukrainian folk belief, pysanka bring luck to the house and protect it from misfortune. To make these special eggs, artists use beeswax, **styluses**, a variety of dyes, and a lot of patience. But the results are beautiful and intricate objects of art. Learn how to make Ukrainian Easter eggs on pages 28–29!

The wax is stored in the tip of the stylus, which looks like a pen. The wax is kept liquid by passing the stylus through a flame every few seconds.

14

Vecheria

On Christmas Eve, children visit their parents and families reunite for the holiday. Traditionally, children brought a dish of food with them to treat their parents on this special evening. The dish, called *vecheria* [ve-CHE-ria] in Ukrainian, was part of a huge feast hosted by the parents for their families. Today, the tradition of vecheria is a way for the whole family to get together and have a nice, cozy Christmas Eve dinner.

This brother and sister are dressed in special hand-embroidered vests to celebrate the Christmas holiday.

A Ukrainian family gathers for a Christmas Eve feast.

The Christmas service

Most Ukrainians are Orthodox Christians. This means they believe in some of the older, more traditional ideas of Christianity. In the Orthodox church, services are conducted the same way they have been for hundreds of years. On Christmas Day, there is a special church service to celebrate the holiday. The priests wear festive robes decorated with silver and gold. The choir sings hymns and carols reserved especially for Christmas. After the service, it becomes a day for enjoying festive food, and for fun, visits, and relaxation.

Sledding is a great way to spend the Christmas holiday.

This angel will travel from house to house wishing all her friends and neighbors a very Merry Christmas.

Koliada

Around Christmastime in Ukraine you'll see bears, witches, pirates, and skeletons parading through the streets, knocking on doors, and wishing people a Merry Christmas. Then, oddly enough, the bears, witches, pirates, and skeletons break out into song, recite a poem, or sometimes even put on a short play. This is the ancient tradition of *koliada* [koh-liah-DAH], or caroling, and it doesn't come cheap! The occupants of each house must reward the carolers, or *koliadnyky* [koh-LIAD-nih-kih], with candy, money, and a warm drink. Children all over Ukraine take part in koliada.

Ready to go caroling? Put on your costume and join these koliadnyky.

Think about this
What holiday do you know of when children dress in costumes and travel from house to house collecting treats? Do you know how this tradition began? Try to find out in your local library.

The Harvest Festival

There is no particular date set for the Harvest Festival in Ukraine. Communities across the country celebrate the harvest as soon as the crops have been gathered and stored, usually in the middle of October. The long, hot summer days are gone by that time, and winter has not yet arrived. The leaves on the trees are turning yellow and orange, and the autumn flowers have begun to blossom— the perfect setting for a party to thank Mother Nature for her many gifts!

Decorations for the Harvest Festival are made from wheat stalks. Wheat is used to make bread, and it is one of Ukraine's main crops. Ukraine is often called the breadbasket of Europe because of its rich harvests.

How did the festival begin?

The Harvest Festival originated thousands of years ago as a way to thank the gods and nature for the abundant harvest. Since the climate in Ukraine is perfect for agriculture, and the soil is the richest in the world, the autumn harvest helped people survive the long winters.

Above: The harvest is a time for great celebration. It is also a time to relax and unwind after spending long hours in the fields.

Right: Bread is the symbol of bounty and prosperity in Ukraine, and huge loaves are baked and presented on special occasions. For the Harvest Festival, the loaf is round and decorated with the sun, wheat stalks, and other symbols of a plentiful harvest.

Ukrainians dress in their festive best for the holiday. Costumes vary from region to region, but they are all hand-embroidered with colorful thread.

Showing off the harvest

The Harvest Festival is usually on a Saturday. The exact details of the festival vary from region to region, but it usually starts with a parade along the streets of the main city. While the parade heads toward an exhibition site, farmers are busy displaying the best of their crops and animals. The exhibition is usually arranged in a stadium or at a fair ground so there is enough room for everybody to gather and enjoy the exhibits. Every farm has its own stand with samples of fruits, meats, vegetables, and drinks. Prizes for the largest fruits and vegetables are handed out by judges at the end of the day.

Dancing a festive circle dance to celebrate the harvest.

Fun and games

After the prizes have been awarded, the fun and games begin. Contests for children are arranged on the festival grounds. The most popular are tug-of-war and sack jumping. On adjacent fields, competitive games, such as soccer, volleyball, or basketball, take place between local teams. Local singers, dancers, and comedians put on fantastic performances that sometimes last until well into the evening. One of the dances that has made Ukraine famous is the **hopak** [hoh-PAHK]. The dancers must be very fit to take part because each movement is quick and requires a great deal of energy.

Two young men dance the hopak. The dance was originally an exercise routine Ukrainian warriors performed to keep fit.

IVANA KUPALA

I vana Kupala is one of the oldest festivals in Ukraine. It is celebrated on July 7th. The tradition of celebrating a midsummer festival began thousands of years ago, when people believed the god of the sun bathed in the river in midsummer. The Ukrainian word *kupala* [KOO-pa-la] means "washing." July 7th is also the day Christians dedicate to John the Baptist. In Ukraine, the two festivals have become one—Ivana Kupala.

Only a bright smile and a floral crown are needed to celebrate Ivana Kupala.

Festival of summer

The fields in Ukraine are filled with flowers in summer. For Ivana Kupala, young girls make crowns out of a variety of flowers and wear them throughout the day. In the evening, when it starts to get dark, the girls make rafts out of their crowns. They place a lighted candle in the center and then let the crowns drift down the river. The crown that floats the farthest will bring its maker luck and success.

You can learn to make a flower crown like this one on page 27.

24

Fire, water, and fun

Several days before the festival, children and adults travel to forests and lakes to practice the traditional circle dances performed on Ivana Kupala. This is an excellent opportunity to get close to nature, and many people bring along a picnic lunch to accompany the fresh air and entertainment. Small bonfires are lit at picnic sites, and everyone jumps over them to cleanse themselves for the year.

According to folk belief, nature's forces focus on plants and herbs on this day, so it is a good time to go herb-collecting. There is also a belief that on Ivana Kupala night, ferns produce a flower that glows in the dark. Anyone who finds the flower can make a wish. Fern-flower search groups forage in the forests for hours. Successful or not, they enjoy the fun.

Swimming is also a popular activity. In the old days, people believed if they washed in the river on this day, they would be purified for the remainder of the year. It is also traditional to splash water on friends—not at all an unpleasant experience on a hot summer day!

Practicing a traditional circle dance for Ivana Kupala.

THINGS FOR YOU TO DO

A round Christmastime, Ukrainian children wear costumes to go caroling. You, too, can wear a costume next time you go caroling. Ask your parents or any adult for old clothes, jewelry, and makeup to fill up your costume box. Let's have some fun!

Be a shepherd!

Wear a long tunic with wide sleeves. Cover your head with a large scarf and wear a headband. Carry a blanket over one shoulder and a long stick in your hand!

Be a devil or a ghoulish ghost!

Wear a red leotard, tights, and gloves, and put on a red devil's mask with horns. Now you are a devil! To be a ghost, wear an oversized white shirt and pants. Cover your face with cold cream and pat on flour. Or wear a scary mask!

Make a flower crown

Do you have any wild flowers growing near your house? If you do, here is a great way to make them into a flower crown, the way Ukrainian children do for Ivana Kupala.

Go outside and pick a bunch of flowers—even dandelions will do. Be sure to pick them with the stems—you will need them. Now you are ready to make a flower crown!

While the flowers are still fresh, take two and connect the stems by twisting them together with the flower buds pointing in the same direction. Keep adding as many flowers as you need to fit the crown around your head. Then connect the ends. If the stems come loose you might have to use some thread to keep the flowers together. Now put on your crown and celebrate summer!

Things to look for in your library

Eggs Beautiful. How to make Ukrainian Easter Eggs. Johalma Luciow, Ann Kmit, and Loretta Luciow (Ukrainian Gift Shop, 1991).

Festive Ukrainian Cooking. Marta Pisetska Farley (University of Pittsburgh Press, 1990).

The Mitten: A Ukrainian Folktale. Jan Brett (G.P. Putnam & Sons, 1989).

Ukraine. Geography Department, Lerner Publications Company (Lerner Publications Co., 1993).

Ukraine. Oleg Harencar (International Video Network, 1993).

Ukraine: its land and its people. Slavko Novitskiy (video).

Ukraine Under Perestroika. David Maples (Macmillan, 1994).

MAKE EASTER EGGS

T wo types of Ukrainian Easter eggs, krashanka and pysanka, are exchanged as small gifts among family members and friends on Easter. Using these instructions, try making krashanka yourself. Everything you need is available in most stores.

You will need:
1. Eggs
2. A spoon
3. Food coloring
4. A cloth
5. 3 teaspoons of vinegar
6. Crayons
7. 3 bowls
8. A pot
9. Water

1 Boil eggs in a pot for 10 minutes. Have an adult help you with this.

2 Fill 3 bowls with water and add a spoonful of food coloring. Put 1 teaspoon of vinegar in each bowl.

3 Draw designs on one egg at a time, using different colored crayons.

4 Put a decorated egg on a spoon and gently place it in one of the bowls of dye.

5 Remove the egg after about 2 minutes and let it dry on an old cloth. Do the same steps with the other eggs.

MAKE STRAWBERRY KYSIL

A popular dessert in Ukraine is *kysil* (kih-SIL). Kysil is usually eaten after lunch or dinner. It can be made with almost any kind of berry, but strawberries are the best!

1 Place strawberries and 2 cups (500 ml) water in the pot. Boil the fruit on high for 1 minute. Then reduce the heat to low and allow the fruit to simmer uncovered for about 10–15 minutes or until the fruit is tender.

2 Push the strawberries through the sieve with a wooden spoon. Collect the juice in a mixing bowl.

3 Stir in sugar. Return the fruit to the pot and boil over high heat for 2 minutes.

4 Reduce the heat to moderate and stir in the dissolved potato starch. Cook for another 2 or 3 minutes, stirring until it thickens slightly.

5 Cool to lukewarm, and refrigerate for 4 hours before serving. Then enjoy a delicious treat.

GLOSSARY

Communist, 16	A person who believes the state should own everything so that everyone can be equal.
hopak, 23	An energetic Ukrainian dance developed by ancient warriors as an exercise routine.
koliada, 19	Caroling.
koliadnyky, 19	Carolers who dress in costumes.
oblasts, 4	States. There are 25 oblasts in Ukraine.
Orthodox, 10	Christians who believe in an older, more traditional form of Christianity.
Paska, 13	A special decorated loaf of bread eaten at Easter.
schedrivka, 10	Wishes of wealth and health at New Year's.
Slavic, 4	The people of Eastern Europe who speak a Slavonic language, such as Polish, Russian, or Ukrainian.
styluses, 14	Small, pointed instruments used to make Easter eggs.
vecheria, 17	A dish children give to their parents on Christmas Eve.

INDEX